How Do You Answer?

Poems
by
Norma Hodges

PublishAmerica

Baltimore

First printing

ISBN: 1-4137-1225-8
PUBLISHED BY PUBLISHAMERICA, LLLP
www.publishamerica.com
Baltimore

Printed in the United States of America

For Donna Biffar,
my favorite poet

Table of Contents

Previously published poems from this manuscript:

"All Cheer," River King Poetry Supplement
"Home Time, Romare Beardon, 70," River King Poetry Supplement
"Fireflies," River King Poetry Supplement
"You Left," River King Poetry Supplement
"Passage," River King Poetry Supplement
"Conversations With a Barn," River King Poetry Supplement
"Both Ways," River King Poetry Supplement
"My Brother Was An Only Child," River King Poetry Supplement
"How Do You Answer," Moon Reader
"To Bob," River King Poetry Supplement

ALL CHEER

The year the earth was hard early
and hoboes came to dine on the porch
and hoe a row for seconds of cherry pie
we drove up prison hill. FIREWORKS
proclaimed the fireworks stand
displaying packages that were their
own advertisement and decoration
in sweeps of exotic colors
explosions against waxy red, orange,
metallic gold, dragons, tigers
springing from the black of night
we'd not see through.

Grospapa, who seldom fetched his
wallet from the bureau drawer,
burst forth, and while we held
choices brave or cowardly, ordered
high pieces, placed for
the proprietor's hairy arm,
bottle rockets, fountains, shooting stars
and necessary punks and sparklers.

We cheer for the fourth of July with
stories so familiar the elderly
spoke in code.

Down the alley a century dropped
away in a sea of blue bells, spiked
red japonica, lily of the valley
spread to the coolness of aged brick.
They partied in July with
red white and blue, Japanese lanterns
glowing across the porch, floating

around the yard to the persimmon tree,
shared by family and the fire station
the old man enticed onto his corner lot.

It was his birthday and honored him,
as well the day.

Father spoke reverently of a
house, waterfront, with a wishing well,
beneath a hill, where they spread
blankets, set out chairs at night
to watch the men row mid-river,
to see his grandfather, splendid,
cast for his bushy eyebrows, blackbeard,
rise in devil's suit and light
fireworks to be doubled in black water.

The climax came the year
the boat caught fire and all dove in
to swim ashore.

We woke and waited for the crack
and bang of early risers,
begged to go softly, saving
the larger ones for later.
Our brick sidewalk didn't blacken
as well as the one
across the street from quiet snakes
that grew from small cones
quickly crisping
to rise, fall, and tumble off
all spent.
from brother inventions
placed to tear
or combinations of louder, louder

HOW DO YOU ANSWER?

light and wait
to throw, to explode
mid-air.

The drive to the country is full of dust
and tangles. Grandpa's yard's deeply
shadowed. We name the cars to distract
Mother's comb. She mourns the lawn.
'When Mother was alive, there were flowers.'

Sisters gather to compare their cakes
and pies. Jars of thick cream wait.
Harrys said they'd bring the ice.

Cousins gather, know where to hide,
how to ride a horse standing up,
how hairs from horses tails grow
to snakes in water troughs.

Fathers waft up from the cellar
in cigar smoke.
identifying laughter and cool air.
Mothers chide, where are your shoes
and what did you get in your hair.   ·
They recall baskets prepared
for Tucker's grove where neighbors came
for a game of baseball, sack races,
tables piled with potato salad, pickles.
Do you remember Mamie's pies
Nobody'd eat Mamie's pies

Back to heat reflecting streets.
Wait for sunset, wash your hands and feet
Grospapa's stationed where the flag had hung
We circle sparklers, lights sizzle,

glitter, drop off into night,
fountains red, then white. then blue.
Each placed and lit to appreciation.
Get a hammer and a nail. The pinwheel
sputters, a darkened wait, faint glow,
one catches and then another, whirls.
Little balls of fire plop.

His glasses glow gold and dragons
hiss. Their breath smells of hunter's
shells, they rise and roar, belly's moist
the red cape reaches like a whip.
The crack barely clears the air before
thunder tumbles all the chairs
and scares the mice, their little feet
beat from across the street.
His horns are shadows, can not see his face.

They laugh and cry "Imagine, - Rain!"
odor of damp earth and the
smell of sheets.

SUMMER CLAD

Fast slivers of light
they land and become goldfinch
their short beaks pulling thistle seed
one.
 after
one.
They line the chain
that holds the feeder
slender feet balancing
auric bodies
following
tiny steps
a quick turn
to upside down.
They are
far more agile
than a month ago
when they were
merely brown.

WILD THINGS

Emerging spears of wild lilies climb the bank
create a path to turn gold in July.
Now tender green leaves
shade the trunks, the shattered branches
They are a mist above the fallen pine, walnut trees,
and forgotten leaves that have lain
submerged by seasons,
sinking through haphazard weaving.
Years ago a gray house sat
near enough to be responsible
for order among the firs
for that bare skeleton
a great tree trunk, a frozen statement
rising over all
surviving tornadoes that
splintered wider targets.
The fence offers a NO TRESPASSING sign,
 but an invitation to adventurers

that cross the roads, the fields to
return to their wilderness
where wood chucks, raccoons,
possums, rabbits and squirrels
appear to be in no hurry
but disappear immediately.
Woodpeckers work by day.
Owls call at night.
The deer, young, long nosed
come near
making nervous inquiries,
their thin legs quickly taking them
beyond curiosity deeply into the tangle.
Twice today a raccoon crossed the yard
a dusky diamond patterned snake
crossed the driveway - for what?
They will not find anything like it
further on.

VISITING GRANDCHILD

She didn't know that snow
came so quietly or so completely
or of its conversations with the sun
that all the brightness could sparkle
in multicolored lights on leaves and branches
to be a distant glowing field.

She didn't know
that unwrapping a candy cane down the lane
would take so long in mittens that left lint
with sticky sweetness and minted fragrance
or that returning on the bentwood sled
her cousins resurrected
would smooth the labored tracks.

OF A GREY CAT AND WILD ROSES

Yesterday the beagle claimed
he must have freedom to protect me.
I let him out the door
then saw a great grey cat
body sleek, shoulders rotating
walk, one paw deliberate after the other
denying any need to hurry
proceeding mid-road
larger than he.
He was almost upon her before she turned.
They disappeared.
Did he know this was no declawed pussycat?

When I took my walk
he came from behind
head high
bounded past
indicating he'd had a fine chase
and bore no battle scars.

Today the bird bath is full of last night's rain.
Wild roses are spreading
simple pink petals with golden centers
proclaiming independent breeding.
We'd feared the county had destroyed
those of the roadside with gravel
but now their bright pattern stretched
from one fence post to the next
bumblebees feeding from the cups

and there
mid-road inverted
Who would have thought her underside
was that beautiful
the cat striped white and grey
She appears more defined
delicate in death
The beagle sniffs
She's very wet.
Sometime before the rain
she did not turn fast enough.

EQUATION

Nine months make
Siamese twins
Wide eyed they reach
to grip each other
and deny that what is
shared is tragedy

    Those wedded
    fifty years
    to the assimilation
    of give and take
    atrophy from the conflict
    of strength and weakness
Siamese twins separated
early breathe
a sigh that all
is there but
cry in loneliness wonder
what was lost

    each wedded leaves a
    thought untended
    secure the other
    can express it
    perhaps supply its
    conclusion

    And

    if one should die
    far away
    silence falls
    within
    the other

HOME TIME, ROMARE BEARDON, 70

The glowing black
of all colors
He is the denial of insistent sweetness
Pale
outside the window
the black that burns
into the annealed slate of his room
the sparkle of cat
the bed posts
created of bold placements
the dull blue that heals cracked walls
that offers eerie illumination
in his dark corner
But his hand is alive, borrowed
from some publication
a worker's
hand shaped about
the absence of a skin drum
resonant singing alive and commanding
controlled by the listening fingers of
his left hand
the beat of being

a beat drained of the long hand beyond
disembodied elegant gesturing a last note
empty of its pick
beyond their bright checkered plane
where the minute black cat
stretches spindly legs
borrowed from the stove's
sharp legs
the memory of lace
spilling from a chest
Pristine, unaware of the quilt
redolent
Its colors an after-image of generations
a stale reminder wandering
above the checkered cloth
to stay the interrupted body
of the bony hand

LOVE AND DEATH

It is the season of new life
the beagle's step is interrupted
climbing banks
scratching into clumps
where new grass rises
through the dead

I saw him yesterday
trotting by the porch
two limp legs dangling
long and furred
from his mouth
It is the season of bunnies

Later, mouth clamped
I saw two delicate ears
protrude beyond his jaws
His dog steps relaxed but purposeful

Near evening
at the porch door
he nosed folded furniture
before joining
our exit

I returned alone
and found
one small mouse
mid floor
looking dazed and damply ruffled
I did not move him

In time of quiet pleasure
he nudged the mouse
from a corner

They walked beside the window frames
mouse first
his wiry legs dutiful
The beagle's tail wagged
faster faster
Mouse
Do you know You are loved

INTRUDERS

How does he perch in undefined air
a jewel, cardinal flown into the rich green
of early morning May
Unheeded calls of an irate dog
Sharp footprints tell the uninvited came
claiming the birdbath dumping the feeder
wandering within my unwilling mind
until morning and recognition

How and where could a snake that large enter
Not the striped one that make quiet u's
along the garden wall and departs
twining through grass
but puddled within these walls
shining like dark spilled syrup
splotched with black
tail inert, head small
intent upon the beagle who found him
announces him loudly
warns every movement

I pull up a chair
there's nobody around who might pick him up
Black plastic bags are too personal
perhaps too fragile
if he fell loose he'd hide   .

Finally
A BOX
He seems to welcome the interference
and moves in
Held beneath the bristles of a broom
are those rattles
or the beating of the captured's heart
I take him to deep grasses
between house and field

CONTROL

sestina

Now she controls the water's flow
its warmth and freshness bubbling
down the Blakean cave where she slept
between chest and knees for forty years.
Rounded shoulders, spine, she'd missed them
and whispers "there now, don't you struggle."

The girls who came complained he'd struggle
his balance shaky swept by the flow
of cheerful words that came bubbling
against his helpless flail, til he slept
away the anxiety of unbalanced years.
In whispers they speak piously of "them."

If she'd said, "They say" he'd ask of "them"
and she would struggle
to identify her carefree flow
of ideas that had been bubbling
randomly about her mind that slept
during his dominating years.

Followed by the he and she of years
of wandering independently of "them"
to clarify their reasoned struggle
to unite imaginations, the flow
with solutions, deep bubbling
of excitement that seldom slept.

There within his mind, it all slept
insipidly awakening through years.
Petty thievery taking from them
mind, body control without struggle,
spread fingers not stemming the flow,
head echoing the hollow bubbling

awakens to the whirr of motors bubbling
while the high computer slept
small machines summate the years.
stacks of printed sheets join them,
sap the man, the mind, of struggle
left behind the mortal flow

that connects the flow ever bubbling
of creations that slept through computed years
arranged all of them, damned the struggle.

EDWARDIAN CHRISTMAS

Not accustomed
to clothing suitable
for display
nor winter nights
white stockings letting
the chilled air creep in
Mother and daughter climb the steps
up the hill where Indians once
shot arrows
into the fort below

Mother and daughter enter
Long white the most modern building in town
the company club house
crushed by heavy doors
ringing from the thump and clatter
of the bowling alley
They have been preparing for Christmas
The first landing brass banister curved
smooth above art-deco lines
radiating speed
the click of billiard balls
from felt tables

Tonight they will see Santa Claus
in the flesh
following weeks of
a right old and jolly self
the hand carved nutcracker
Tiny Tim
brave sacrifices
Mary
tired

waiting
rising
to the hall bedrooms who knows for whom

The tree beyond the balcony rises lit and tinseled
The piano pulled from the wall
hides a DECK THE HALLS pianist
as they descend the steepest steps

HO HO HO a red suit, shining hood shading
his cheesecloth face out of
newspapers black and white
flaming from the fire
of KKK
Satan
the cotton thick on his chin
blank eyed
moving the line
"Have you been a good girl"
He knows but gives to every one
a net stocking
lumpy

Boxes
piled beneath the tree are left
for children who need them
Sick and pale they will come
from gray clusters a block away
where they skip school
and shoot shafts of light
from hand held mirrors
into classrooms
far below
At least one of them will open a dime store box
the game Mother wrapped

put it on the bare floor of their dark room
and spin the arrow with
trembling hands

FIREFLIES

Beneath
steady stars
fireflies
trail across the meadow
rise into the five trees
that separate
field from mowed land
a flashing hoard
punctures its
deeper darkness
as they beckon to
a love who
answers
stitching in
and out of branches
Do blue pretenders
fly among them
pulsing
silent songs of prey
do they collide
mid air
and these
who arc
toward me
abdomens
dimming
are they
tired
or
escaping

THE VISIT

The frame house no longer
heard slammed doors
or felt the muddy boots of children
urged in from cold
or hands that left traces of ripe apricots.
Alma answered
a cousin called from memory
blue eyed, glasses, hair orderly
She had done so many things
to her hair with ribbons, plastic fasteners
rollers, every dime store invention
tended fingernails and toes

"I haven't the foggiest," she said
"Dora, cousin, Dora"
"Perhaps it's the hair," she said

When Aunt Eva was alive
they walked right in
and found her at the great black stove
the stove demanding, "Don't touch
check the flu, close the damper
lift the lid, add a few split logs
shake down the ashes"

The beast, angry with heat
dispensed scars to the inattentive
Knew its mistress
was gentle
held cold shoes and feet on the oven door
offered warm water from its well
to add to what the gasping pump would spew
and held kitchen efforts within

until the popcorn popper
 shaken turned
 sputtered to quiet
 announced time to move on

A sister-in-law had carried
food in from God's Portion Day
Plastic cartons awaited disposal
The teakettle rested on an electric burner
A game was on a television set
so large one expected

tackled men to tumble onto the carpet

She had received letters listing invasions and replacements
 They were thinner but
 moved within the space
 she'd known for them
 Remaining flesh was a miracle
 a rescued memory
 beyond the album where
 she had scratched the eyes from
 every face of their cousin
 other side of the family
 who often arrived to steal attention
 from her

Ned left before they said goodbye
and at the car she saw him bring
Matthew from the barn
the eldest who reminded her
of his mother

She'd forgotten how they gathered
about a departing car for last words
smiling with recognition
of another's secret divulged
and as the prickly child
didn't dare to hold them

THE POEM

She dreamt at eighty she returned
to school
a poem in her womb and
teased it out
Too soon. It became a fortune cookie slip
blood stained, all faded and
wafted off
    to stick upon a wall
The flat-faced girl she once knew
told of her creation, a school bus,
shining thing
It filled the gutted halls
and rolled
to become a threatened caterpillar
pulled into itself
then slowly rose and resumed its
former bloat
But she saw pieces left behind
and saw her poem fall

WHO CALLED

He'll only lie there
spent
and give sad looks across the room
to my attention

but now that I'm up
I can't tell
what was about last night
When he first barked and yelped
I looked

I thought I saw a shadow
hunched
but the bird bath goes first
and it stood
True the low feeder had been raided
lid agape, emptied

One we loved died from exhaustion
two days ago a thousand miles away
she was so gentle
released anger would not
have been spent on a small dog

Were there more than one
He raced from room to room
a hailstorm from his claws
strafed the window glass

Repeated at the door
pleading
"No"
I'd be up all night
waiting for his return

The moonlight poured
through the clear-story
but defined nothing

Was it so large
it shadowed
all belqw

STORM

Last night the news told
no more than what flashed
to light the house, all sides
at once, and shook the firs
to angered roars
Now morning
still unlit
has roused a scattering
of chirps

Centered,
the bird bath
in shards pins leaves
shed of blossoms
awaiting fruit
Yesterday's purple iris
knot colorless and
rose buds, their umbilical cord
bent to suffocate
hang above the tracks
that end with worms
urged to seek the sheltered walk
left
with no return

THE FIRKIN

In the ancient firkin
carefully crafted
Time polished
is the laughter
of children
It waits for the round lid to lift
to divulge
slight figures with unformed eye brows
pale above eyes lit
with the joy of companionship
or brother sister
chosen for attention
a giggle behind little teeth
just a quarter of a barrel
of laughs
It also holds the baby face

squinched against the sun
The glamorous thirties
of sinuous silk draped perfectly
for hot bright lights
black waiting lips
gleaming dreaming
long lashed eyes
missed the life within corduroy
and itching wool
and the blinking eyes
concurrent with the camera click

WIND

No light marks dawn.
The sun is somewhere
in another world
or day, beyond the flat cover
of cloud
pressed down to
panic air that
thrashes above the beagle.
Low
he noses a tangle
of grasses.
The wind is pierced
by shrieks. His prize blind
unfurred is dropped.
He sniffs the culvert
both ends.
a shadow bird held
mid-road
 accepts
small flights
windward.
The grass is flecked
with pebbles
dead white
They are ice.

VERNAL EQUINOX

A few odd drops!
    We ask "Is the
    brief ballet
    of vernal equinox
    just for eggs?"
Atop the hill we meet
the sun squarely
    and turn to find it
    casting our shadows
    down the lane
    The little dog's upends him so
    his tail precedes the flopping ears
I can see the yard greening
grass sneaking beneath
dead winter's bones, lapping
the road's edge and hear
    chicken's voices repeating
    in morning chuckles
    and find
It is the windmill's whine
    Across the field willows
    turned a wild blond
    thrash against the slate sky
      and the rain
      nudges onward

FOG CALLS

I enter
greedy for the
world that's mine.
It waits
a Scottish castle
endless halls
flanked by thistle
candelabra. Clusters of
elderberry fold
into Queen Anne's lace
above indistinct clover.
A rabbit mid-road
creases the soft
white curtain.
Pipers reiterate
waking notes. Gold
the sun
edgeless slices
bright blades through
branches separating
glowing leaves from
the deep of pines
shimmers droplets
of air and me.

APRIL ONE

April one and just past seven
fulfilling what was missed
the nuthatch ascends
A narrow limb quickly
in small leaps
not far from the jay
whose weight bent his branch
it waved to his departure
The doves call up and down the scale
adding punctuation. .

How the lilac promises
its pale green tips swollen
A gathering there, house finch, sparrow, robin
Blue jay plummeting into the lilac's core
Juncos in the new grass
and that wild rabbit
creeping, dark eyes rounded
from his head searching in all direction,
not caring that it's April one?

I look to the northwest
difficult from this window
to follow serious instructions
of one I loved when small
"You will see six snow white doves
carrying a banner
Call me on the phone
and I'll tell you what it said"
I made the call
guilty of missing
what adults know
and he said "April Fool"

and told of how I must
rush to change the sugar bowl
to salt.

MATISSE CLOUDS

Matisse clouds
scattered through the early sky
pale green in waiting
supply the bare trees of April
a sly leafing
Bespectacled he reaches
his long pole
to mark the spectral shades
And those who have joined him
who in life named him
the most magnificent of colorists
nod
as the sun rises
and erases

MATINS

Dear dog
the sun lies to you
with thirty more
before it turns
    He whimpers whines
    His claws clamber
    across the window
We sing in counterpoint
    his coat in readiness
    for pursuit
    and I in preparation
We burst
    upon the chirp
    and calls
    The doves beat off
    and he sits
    lapping the morning dew
        The clover have opened
        fringed purple overnight
        beneath the spreading
        abundance of wild turnip
        its gold barely wakened
        by the fluted notes of the
        red wing blackbird
        and pheasant's departure
        premature, wings and
        expansive tail rattling
        followed by his mate
        just clearing weeds

Intruded
	a wrinkled balloon
	beats in its trap
	between the breeze
	and a silent jet trail feathering
	mocks the sun's slow progress
We return
	I trod the bars
	He trots the beat

MARBLE FLU

She saw them all
whole and glowing
marbles she had owned or wanted
some she had seen destroyed
They were piled inside her
the large pale shooters she lost
They were tumbling
mottled deep hues
blues violets browns
her step-father's treasures
laid away a hundred years ago
A man from farmers market
called those Bennies
trophies from the last clay of the day
browns knowing the depths of firing
and those
She should celebrate
the agates she washed her hands to hold
to see how close to red the stone
would swirl in variations
of brown, orange
swift strokes of amber
How heavy the glass, the clay, the stone
For two days they held her
then she saw the little bubble
A steelie wends its way to air
small
but a beginning

AWAKENING

"Does he talk" they ask
"We communicate"
"How do you communicate"
"It takes a day or two"
He is so quiet
"Is he always this quiet"
"We communicate"
"How do you communicate"
"By repetition of the things we do"
And then he responds to
my kiss and smiles and
it was all worth while
it is so much more than he did
before

The woman next door moans
and people speak to her in
loud voices
"Anna
can you hear us"
"Ness"
it takes a day or two
"How many fingers do you see" "A New'

"Anna can you hear me"
"Ness"
"How many fingers do you see"
"New"

"Anna" "Ness"
"How many fingers -"
"Can't you add"
"Add? Anna? How many fingers?"
"Can't you add! Add one or two!
I get so tired of two!"

WAITING ROOM FOR SURGERY

Eleven of them lying
in puffed white caps
on silver cots
with green for the operating room
smooth white above
Each bed holds
its stunted grey balloon
caught in the steel rods
the line and tubes

Do drifting people watch t.v.
Darkened boxes hang above
They will be the show
selected programs
beeps, numbers, moving lines

The desk lit
    a kiosk
    hardware
    in soft colors
    sand, rose
    and wedgewood blue creeping!
    across the shining floor
    all lit
Coordinated silent people
take silent orders
clipped
beneath steel clips

HOLD THAT TIGER

I thought I'd grow to share
night sounds of parties
up the hill
cars letting off and loading
Those cars with mocking horns
running boards supporting adolescents
clutching window frames
and rumble seats
reached above the laughing heads
of oil cloth girls
decorating spare tires

One summer night
we parked along the hill
beneath a roof party
to hear the orchestra
Daddy plucking banjo
murmurs
feet beating the floor
until the tiger broke away
horns chased screaming until
heads blew off
and flew
balloons all colors
into the night
next day they found them
miles away
wrinkled
and breathless

ABOUT TRAVELING

She said
    It's our first trip away
    Do you find it hard to leave the children
I said
    I find it harder to leave the dog

How so
    With children you give them a calendar
    Mark when you'll return
    Leave favorite food
    Have someone they enjoy in charge
    You promise a surprise
    Send post cards
    Call

    When you return the children say
    What did you bring me
    But
    a large dog knocks you down
    a small one gives you long sad looks

I didn't hear how it went
We didn't know
She'd left hoping for a cure
until we heard
she didn't find it

WILD LILIES

A July dark morning
wild lilies amber against the deep pine trees
shielded in the haze, closed, protected from
the day and rain, but light slashes
reach into dark solemnity
    When the sun shines, will this rich carpet
    impose its starred gaiety across the
    needles of seasons past?
        Will I wake and search
          for this remembered thing?

Years ago when my birthday
fell on Thanksgiving
drowsy, in a stupor
against the seal skin
my great aunt wore
I saw fairies from the car
    "Oh look," my father said
    "a fairy boat" and lit by
    shore lights against the
    black river of late afternoon
    I saw, crowded by cars
    'So large," my mother said
    "they could have a dance on there"
fairies whirling lightly clad
in the chill dark air

DECEMBER TWENTY THREE NINETY NINE

Please
Must I sleep

I am the child
sent to bed
in the middle of adult
enchantment
We will save
something for you
they promise
But I know

the moon can only hold this much sun
for one night
Tomorrow I will mourn
this rich darkness
the glitter beyond fingered shadows

rusted iron
hard and dark
of racing rabbit
against the glowing snow

Night colors
pull forth
the warm blackness
red from
patch of cane
twisted leaves umber
beyond the green of fir

Never have the sharp stark black
 shadows pressed as
deeply as those beneath the lilac bush
a complicated calligraphy
laid upon its cold white page
the child in darkness
writes the words the adult keeps

YOU LEFT

You left so quietly
wrapped
by those who knew
you wouldn't need to breathe
I thought
Now I will sleep your death
I will not worry to wake
to tend you
But the stars were too bright
unblinking unrelenting
I rose and walked the night
You returned
a face cradled by branches
swayed in breezes
I thought
those branches will rearrange
erase you.
But you stayed
Each morning I woke
to find you
still asleep
until the leaves fell

PASSAGE

They're gone

 Three owlets
side by side, six claws
clinging to a mulberry branch
siblings extravagantly tufted
striped more intricately than

tigers grant their young
pressed into a feather bole.
Their elegance did not protect
them from ejection. No longer
fed them. Hooked beaks

scarcely visible between eyes
widely circled, clutched slits
unused to light. Yoruba, African
masks enfold them in inner
darkness. Behind them

the thousand small sounds of
a timber declare twilight's
silence. Bunnies rule the lane.
Feathers expand, soften and
the voice that called the darkness up said
"You're OWL," "You're OWL." "You're OWL.'

DAY ONE

Happy New Year, Joe!
High above the snow he raises a gloved hand
then backs his tractor along the fence to lift
a giant bale of hay
and rumbles down the hill
trailing dried alfalfa

A layer of daylight edges shreds
of clouds across the sky
glows where black Angus intent
upon rough earth nose among stubbles

The sun emerges
bursts a great demanding ball
fringes the pearl of rising clouds
animates the cattle. They cluster
unwind single file behind the tractor

How fast the sun rises
How quickly the world turns
Here's the Rose Parade
Three men in parachutes land
one by one onto a single circle of earth

and I remember California

how we bicycled down a country road
to see the scatter of fragments
from the womb of one small plane
plummet
awaited the count off
the strings rise
and blossoms burst

Steadied they float
and land full grown
to quickly gather up their silken placentae

REUNION 50 FMHS

Desperately gray with a few old dangling
wires. One solitary box protruding
from what had been the office, where
comfort was limited to the steamy
heat that blew through winter. The hollow
sounds, the bounce, the bounce of balls and calls
the shrill whistle. Everyone expecting something
new to happen. But It never did. Yesterday
with gravy. Grow, grow up. They grew

So now she comes to celebrate survival,
and finds that those she thought about
couldn't. She stood marooned until
she saw the ladies gathered, around cheerful tables
chatting and recalled church suppers where
women wore aprons, gifts
she declared nobody wore anymore.
These wore jogging shoes and stirrup pants
All like her a generation older

Her best friend of calls and Christmas cards
handed her a tag. It was a kid party
They pinned past names and faces to their chests
She couldn't see enough to tell who was whom
and aging spouses, new, wore no clue.
Those who were two orbited the other.
They toured empty rooms
Men inquired about her dead brother.

"Charlie, Oh Charlie" He'll answer only Chuck
"Do you remember history?"
They drew cartoons. History
was only war. The boys returned all one age

The girls finished college before
the boys began.

His wife drum major in white boots
with satin chest, whistle clenched in pearly teeth
Come gym teacher crouched intent whistle ready
Don't worry, we sat on facing curbs
waited for permission to cross the street.
Announcements through the pause and chatter
asking that the next be sooner
Perhaps she'll come to wonder how it got so late

CONVERSATIONS WITH A BARN

Henry Miller - I've always looked upon decay
as being just as wonderful and rich an
expression of life as growth

I hear the barn from the road
wagon loads of hay
miik drawn from cows hissing into
buckets, the stomp and snort of
horses, their gnawing wearing down
rounding feed boxes. An owl
somewhere high trades its calls with yonder.
I hear boards the length of
trees applaud the wind,
slip down

Now
    snow has flattened the brush
raised a path to the wide gate.
Diminished wood gapes a horizontal
entry. The barn stands square. Seen
from the road it's shadowed. Here,
ice pales to snow, there is
no interior. I thought I'd ask
"May I intrude?" but enter as
the early sun, unbroken snow.

A dark rope dangles
from the sharply
pitched roof.
Bleached boards too worn to
be the work of man are pauses
in a song of winter fields.
We speak of different things. The voice

is neither passionate nor distant.
Where words are gifts
I hold them, go lightly, but hear
"You think you're old!" You don't know
what old is." and say
"I'll be back."

THE GARDEN

It was
a year of garden
summer deeply
into fall
When butterflies
gathered about
the gold chrysanthemums
to hoard
the shortened sun
Now winter
holly calls
to harps of branches
iced by cold night air

ALARM

If I rise, I will fillet myself
my backbone still among the sheets
and take with me half the dream
unfinished
    the problem
how to feed all the unknown
I invited to eat and nobody looks
the same
I think I asked the one and
didn't know she'd bring three kids,
no four,
they're hiding in the dark
I rise
in disconnected stability and
leave them all in the
sheets

MICRO BURST

Some
who were outside
knew to hurry
Some pulled their cars
from the road
left them and hid
Nurseries gathered tots
into tiny rooms
Some watched confident it would pass
though a shivering dog did not know
of the end of it
of the length of turmoil
as the geometry of roofs enlarged
chasing displaced shingles across the yard

Trees
trunks bent and streaming coifs
held near the ground snapped
in splinters
broke the earth with all the tentacles of life exposed
trees, that had survived while those
who planted them had moved or died
trees, that fought from seed
for the crowded timber floor

The fine architecture
of old barns failed
The aisles, roof supports , beams
the proud four square shafts were relegated to rubble
Rolled grain bins
crumpled as paper tossed away
not fit to be read again

That evening
across the wide meadows
fireflies rose and pulsed
a strange flowing rhythm

In the days that followed
yard lights
once hidden within growth were restored
among miles of leafless broken stubs

The people who counted exclaimed
"No one was hurt!"
and there was silence

INTRUSION

Somewhere he dropped a week or so
lifted without respect
and left a dark and gaping hole
whose healing stretched and paled
so others hardly saw, but
oozed within his head
spoiling blessed certainty
and simpered beneath the thin bone walls

CALIFORNIA CHILDREN

California children came in winter
were intrigued by leafless trees where
birds rest among the vacated nests of last spring
follow creek beds of raw earth and stones
passing incurious cattle and used
the lawn tractor for trips across the yard
They watched hawks hovering, beating their wings
above the stubbled fields, descend swiftly toward
the animal life that scavenges corn

They collected the things they'd need
and packed them among the clothes they'd worn
Amish lunch boxes, a cow jawbone, milkweed pods
real flint and the dried globes of Chinese lantern seed.

SMALL CHAIRS

People think she collects
small chairs
not knowing she holds
the ghosts of children

I
That low rocker was
an apology to child number one
for number two
who took to walking
while his legs were very short
They became bowed
She built the seat up
upholstered it
with the nubbly red she liked
He rubbed graham crackers into the seat
He always had a cold
Could not get the gist of rocking
and grew into a larger chair
Red too
After spills and a bloody nose
they sawed the rockers off
The others
How they fill the room
Each accepting the chairs in turn
Respectful of big brother

II
This one's a Christmas gift
She accepted regally
Caressed the knobs and turns
Posed ankles crossed
Invited little neighbors in to sit

on the floor
She made sure the door
was open when she left the room
Moved only within sight of them
One day she sat too near the fire
The paint blistered
and it was never the same

III
The school chair
deep red with yellow stripes
seat worn smooth
under the scrutiny of
Stand. Speak up. Sit down
while at their desks those better prepared
waved frantically
to be next

IV
And that rocker's a centerpiece
Mother bought for the living room
hoping her straight haired daughter
would fit
But she couldn't read and rock
All legs she
Sprawled across the rug
Now and then
rocked it with her foot
keeping time to the radio

V
This one sits quietly
understated
back splayed
His mother put his father out
He awaits instructions
He's dressed like Mickey Mouse
short dark pants, red tie beneath his chin
he's spread a handkerchief
across the seat
He's considered a fine example
taps on his toes
heels hung on the rungs
He dreams he's Fred Astaire

VI
The simple straight backed
wasn't for a child
but from her mother who said
"protect it"
Great grandmother's chair
who didn't have to lift the babies far
The sturdy family men
descended from Green Mountain Boys
preferred their women small
Mother sang her song
"My kitty, my kitty
my poor little kitty'
Father shuddered
said she slid into her notes
Mother taught the song
Insisted on repetition
until the slide was
exactly right.

IMELDA'S FASHION SHOW 79

She arrived rain drenched
in stained tourist white
reeking
Assumed an air of nonchalance
leaving prints of barrio across
the freshly tended lobby of the Manila Hotel
Now hot water climbs seven floors
to snake through her hair and all she wears

Merlyn led the team of them, exuberant
from the hall
inspired by Imelda's words, one boy three girls
dark eyed with tawny skin, and trim
Today they wore navy slacks and gold blouses
of friendly print accessorized
It is the Tuesday costume
Each day they dress in clothing designed
to prod the poor to emulate

The barrio was sunk in mud
a garbage dump once
it is now and more
Unclad children watched from doors
The team floated over all
in golden boots and matching hats
A chapel held no promises
warm and damp
aisles ordered by long board seats
children entered in bits of cloth
One was tied in lacy blue
Babies clung above mother's pregnant bellies
and young walkers clutched and cried
for a ride

Children guarded what they have to give
a little blood for raisins
Five sticks of gum rated
over dried fruit

Over what the foreigner might learn
who looked for "dry eye"
that would progress to bitot spots
to blindness
Though their skin is rough
the stunted starved may not grow
beyond control, but those who survive
on rice alone have A deficiency

The tests they take are
what do you see and smell and taste
and can you close your eyes
and stand
This time around the losers win
and get the "A"

Thunder roars through the lobby
and from the gaping elevator
mouth wide, the electric green eyes of a lion appear
Children collapsed on lobby chairs rise
He shakes his shimmering mane
whips the tasseled tail
Drums beat. Cymbals clang. He rears
drops to the floor, paws the air comically
IT'S HAPPY HOUR

Here centrifuges rock the twilight room
of wooden floors and transomed doors
windows deeply silled
widely framed

Above the earth Merlyn, in efficient white,
tells of small cells that held GIs who died
and left the lab a shadowed place
Water flows from unattended taps
typewriters clack messages no one can see

Tomorrow
she will wear
the eggplant blouse
with avocado trim
relieved by patterns of peach
into the barrio
The bloods will fly
to distant labs
She prays they'll meet

ANANDA

She was blond
a combination of two fine breeds
but mainly to herself
she watched the gravel road and tended
what wandered in

or wandered off and
brought home a lumbering possum
Laying the limp body on a mound
she withdrew to await
his resurrection
then returned him to his bier
until boredom overtook her

She attended lost kittens
A beagle pup found her a willing mother
They dislodged rabbits from roots and leaves
and chased them
Her step made three of his
She took prey quietly
The beagle's excitement rang
through the woods

Beagle custody was arranged
down the road
he would be named "Fred'
by an elderly lady who exercised daily
Ananda bisected the leash
and led him away with her teeth

When the pace wearied her
she devised a series of circles
through culverts
 disappearances
 fresh returns
Nudged them both with her broad nose
for recognition of her cleverness

Then something grew within her
and she lay beneath his window
in winter's dried flower bed
rang the bell
He brought stale bread laid out for birds
dead rabbits

She would not accept his gifts
He leaves his scent for her
on her bank
watches the window

BEYOND THE GYRO-CART

Just beyond where Nick tends the gyro-cart
silly sparrows
spilled from their nest:
prance on tender feet
pink almost transparent
Can they support a sparrow's weight

Beneath the newly feathered bodies
there is something wiry perhaps electric
about them
Do young sparrows eat gyro meat
The crumb laid out carefully has waited
Crumb
It is wider than the sparrow's head but he
takes it all
rises from his new feet
spreading his short wings
and flies

BOTH WAYS

I saw a shadow cross the road
too far ahead to know,
absorbed by trees
shattered logs, pine cones
and crumbling leaves with
just a skiff of snow
fallen in the night
that showed he ran
on shapely bear clawed feet
though hard to tell
and returned on steps
so closely paced
they almost matched
the ones that came

WILD TURKEY

He strode across the lawn
with more power and propriety
than a peacock
strong legs commanding the earth to move him
His long neck and head
pointing to a destiny far ahead

Body deeply feathered
I longed for a seduction
to see the blue rising to his head
but most of all to see that great tail spread

and thought of Flannery's peacocks
forty at one time
How the priest would call
eager for their display
and would sit for hours
staring at them

YOU HAVE SWALLOWS

I see you have swallows she said
They're very desirable
eat lots of bugs
and once you have them they'll return
And they do
opening like starfish
with rose tipped breasts and dark wings
the vee of pointed tails
focussing on their shaggy pockets
glued below the eaves
pile excrement on iris leaves

to produce a row of greedy beaks
quivering yellow rimmed gaping
unaware that they're taking turns
from the round bodied patience
that warms them

They appear
not yet colorful
unsteady
braced on shingles
in independent disorder

and then one day
like starfish
they dip before the doorway
and disappear

MY BROTHER WAS AN ONLY CHILD

I saw him last, head turned
to smile at me in sleep. I wasn't
prepared for the intimacy.
His undertaker was a friend.
At his feet were exotic flowers.
We'd done the same for our mother
two years before. The extravagance,
a denial of hospital gowns.
Had pleased us then.

When he died Bill was everywhere,
the group that shared the altar years before
when he married his second wife,
Ibby, pretty daughters, step children,
teachers, students, friends old and new
The minister told of long talks they had. How
he lost track of time listening
to tales of Bill's boyhood.
He said, "Bill was an only child."

The month before, I'd crossed the state
to have three days with him.
Thin, ambulatory now and then.
He tasted fruits he had requested
but could not swallow. He accepted
the spikey birds of paradise
I'd struggled to get on the plane.
He apologized for childhood pranks
I had thought he'd done in innocence.

Apologized for demanding
we share my first bicycle
and insisting it have the bar
to protect his masculine dignity.
I said "It hadn't mattered."
He said, "Oh yes 'it had!"
I said it wasn't my first bicycle."

Three years before our father
rescued one for me
and with his skill and patience
made it new
shiny red, perfectly white striped
and then suddenly the town
was mine to wander.
A boy on a blue bike pulled up
"What kind of bike is that?"
And I sped off knowing it had no brakes.
The seat wedge always bruised me
when I jumped down to stop.

And Bill remembered.
Now he invited me into
Uncle Herman's dusty barn
(the realm of men) where
Dad lifted him into its grey rafters
to bring down
Herman's gift to his daughter
years and years before
when ladies
came to gentle stops.
It had ornate dress guards
of darkened cord
and when he touched them
they disintegrated from age.

THE CRITIC

The sun emerges glowing
discloses what the night has left
a world softened white

The fence wires, posts
all weeds and trees shimmer
yet there atop the oak
still and dark
is one great black crow
surveying the frosted country

IT'S THERE IT'S THERE

Why across the blue hills
where yard lights glow between pines
is there one flashing light
repeating its glare
marking off a modicum of area
because it is distant
because it is small
the hills swollen with snow
now glow more white
than the ground glass sky
of rose and blue

What winter lightening bug waits
for my eyes to droop
what nervous herald of something new
of a snow bound evening
to claim
claiming
the glow of drifts the black of branches
and here and here and here
it says

HOW DO YOU ANSWER

How do you answer
when
    a ghost
    calls
    your name
Do you step
    into
    the dark
    night and watch
    it grey
    between
    cricket calls
or wait at the t.v.
judging all the voices
Do you phone friends to see
    if
they're still alive
or
    turn off the light and wait

THE RETURN

It wasn't an attractive place
of dreams
but familiar
along a shore
where buildings had eroded
to a measuring of rooms
in sand

There were people
preoccupied
waiting
A woman said this was about me
It was a presentation
I was not to worry
about what
or whom
She placed me in a vast and sunken room
poorly lit
floor curved to the center

Against a wall a group of men
waited
dressed in dull suits
felt hats
and with a nod one broke away
small, just my height
came to me
held me
kissed me
long and deeply, knowingly

I woke wondering
Who would kiss me
with such assurance
and then I knew

TO BOB

I thought when you died
I'd remember my fine companion
The miles we walked
Sunday morning breakfasts
of your imagination
bicycling, spreading our coats
to sail before the wind
and forget the helpless years
supporting you through the shower
feeding you
hooking up the formula
regulating the flow
but now
I remember kissing your stiff lips
mouth wide to enfold them
your word "uv" forced
between our worlds

TSUNAMI

I try to gather up the pieces.
Was it the owl night?
When the children and I
watched their great shadow bodies
fill autumn air
searching sailing over the orchard

I've tried to gather up the pieces
You left the five of us
but wrote each day on the envelope paper
that we shared

Your letters are somewhere
diminished by a rubber band.
Something you needed to do
a nutritional survey of Malasia

The children were more entertaining
than disciplined, but kind.
I wondered which round head
warm and huddled close
might think of the owl balls
among pine needles
with tiny bones woven through them

Sleep was a feast
a reward of a day completed,
accepted
a trusted burial,
until
something was withdrawn,
or added
a sound

or an absence of sound
a blinding light
more white
more bright
than bearable

Metatron stood
tense and still beside my bed
yet in motion
light bursting from every pore of his body

About his eyes
was there a rim of red?
the pain
beyond any shame
of his
unclothed body?

Now discovered
Why would he not disappear
allow the merest retreat.
I willed him gone
concentrating
but he stood severe before my ignorance
Frail, by comparison, I watched
pain deform you into
this human form half a world away and
in our mute language cried
"Bob's on fire." He faded then

Off the coast of Kota Bahru
on a holiday, romp in the ocean
More water than fire
Tsunami, a tidal wave raised
from volcanic depths.

A letter said you were all right
and by week's end I heard from you
How two young men had been lost
of your great sorrow
How you had been rescued
and who rescued you

We talked for many years
of many things
but not of that
You never said you came to me.
I never asked.

FLOOD

Another day of near dawn
when the damp air
soaks away the sun
and morning waits
through darkening
skies for the roar
and flash that
may clear the air,
that crumpled leaves
may dry from leggy
branches and
swell a bud and lift
the fallen aster.
Another day, down below,
where men had
tried to claim
the fields in
simpler days,
the swirling river
ate away the dykes
and tore
from flooded houses
sogged on the other side,
with one great sucking gulp,
water enough to spew across
its reclaimed bed
with the sound of
locomotives, nearing
bearing down
shattering window panes
in passing.

g
n
i
go
EP
KE
EY
TH
NE
GO
BE
ULD
SHO
EY
TH
INK
I TH
EN
WH
ST
JU
AND
NG
LO
TOO
ARE
EY
TH
ES
AK
SN
KE
LI
NT
DO
I

THE CLIPPING

There it is
yellowed
a memory she can not share
a small Iowa town
January five seventy seven
with her mother's message
"A little snow for you"

Central Park
the smallest detour home
from a Sunday matinee
across the park
beyond scraped sidewalks
snow comes above her shoes

She escaped home without
the crippling weight of boots
to share the stiffening cold within
this island within the cast iron fence
the frozen pond

Beneath her mother's handwriting
is the simple fence,
small trees within
a monument of rounded stones rising into
a snow capped tower
a medieval cylinder
What small thing if not a dried brown soul
could live within those walls

 Some years before she saw the park
healed of interruption
one moment
travelling from somewhere
to someplace else

Fish ponds in small towns
become ugly things
Float discarded wrappers
dead fish inverted
a lifeless bird

Yet here, still snow covered
more isolated than Saint Finbar's
or William Tell's
the yellowed paper
is her chapel

ALMOST NINETY FOUR

Once he thought going
Downstairs was descending
Step
By
Step
Into the basement
A room of over flow
And occasional flooding
Until the choice
Was removed
And flying
He was transformed
Into a puzzle piece
Deeply bruised confused
Plugged in
His hands search for
Tubes
While he waits through days of
Anxious faces
A friend who can not hear
Listens
And wonders if a bruise has made
His voice musical, a flute rising
Oboe, deep and pleasing
A whisper "Let's get out of here"

THE REDHEADED GIRL

There's haze today
where yesterday's buds held tight
asleep encrusted
and winter birds
clutched bare branches to reflect
the morning sun off snow
and glow
the cardinal, purple finch
jay, small neatly drawn junco,
chickadee

My youngest came. They said he would,
And then
I felt the near warmth
of his scrutiny
We touched
He trembled so, I said, "My land
is something wrong?"
He lied

He opened up my hand
and smeared the cool perfume
of lilacs on and in between each finger
so they turned palm up
to reach for spring

For the opening to the promise of
buds unfolding
the twisting wind whipping
writhing branches to green
What was bare and clear
evolved a glistening complex thing

and I glimpsed fair white skin
strawberry hair lost
in a burst of spreading
deeply clustered
lilacs

RE UNION

They arrived by plane
and rental cars
and strolled in
from just beyond the hill
Brought warmth and murmur
assorted voices
pierced by sudden laughter

When evening came they gathered
on the lawn to salute the departing sun
with bubbles children twisted
from plastic rings
glowing clusters
banners of
quivering iridescent giants
The bubbles stumble
on a blade of grass
splinter mid-air
leave empty circles
on smooth surfaces
wander into leafy trees

Winter reveals their sparkle
on the bared branches
and when the sun is low
we hear the murmur
feel the warmth
of what is missing

GRANDDAUGHTER

She comes to collect what she needs to sleep
The small delicately flowered quilt from home
with three plush cats gathered above it
she wears the sleeveless over-tunic
she designed for third grade medieval studies
properly long for maidens but lacking sides
Peacock blue, it contrasts with her shadowed flesh
Her amber hair is tangled from the water-balloon
she broke over her head this morning
when

Joyously celebrating the intrusion
        she leashed the willing beagle
        Gathered a bottle of bubbles and the loop
        that spread them into an iridescent ghost
        On the lawn, dog ahead, she unwound them all
        The strange apparition flowed out and off
        from her wild axle
Now the maiden requests the tape of an unrecognized
princess
It is where she left it after its fourth showing
She arranges herself in a deep chair
beneath her cover

SOUNDS OF NINETY SEVEN

Hear the voices of children
The breathy whisper
the confident
the clown
Hear the baying beagle
cross the yard
meadow
field

Pheasant's wings pummel the air
Hear the feathered call of an owl
Hear the space lab span
the three minute universe
of our evening vision
Hale Bopp's disappearance
into the silent night

MY MOTHER MY CHILD

In the beginning all was fine
then you said "children are like puppies
cute, but they tend to grow"
and you grew another puppy
Mama's boy and Daddy's girl

I thought I had the finer bargain
and learned how to catch a ball
keep basketball scores
You thought my legs were too long
but I could really run
and Mama's boy climbed up
to watch the beaters go
taste the dough

You said I must never lie
stand up straight
keep clean
You said you never went
with a boy you wouldn't marry
I said I hadn't gone with one
I'd marry yet
In time I did.

We brought our daughter home
for Easter
I'll buy four dozen eggs I said
You said I'd need just one
It was slight of hand
Child prodded found egg
Put it in the basket
Grandfather slipped one out
rehid it for the game

I'd bragged at school
of fifty eggs
Wondered who had eaten
My fine provisions

Years passed
our family grew
Daddy died
You married a friend
He died too
You arrived by bus softly gray
a real live Mother
with a box of plants to share
your yard with ours

And then there was helplessness
You were cared for in a home
I held you
You'd become so small
I read you accounts of Easters
I had written
read of the discovery of deception
your pale eyes brightened
you glowed
"You never knew," you asked
I said "I never knew

What can I get for you
what would you like?"
"MONEY," you crooned
"It's not allowed, you know"
but saw you could barely hear
couldn't walk or see to read
"I'll get you some," I said

I brought you a packet
of dollar bills
You sighed
"That's a lot of money"
held it close
"You'll have to hide it," I said
"Oh I will
I surely will"

BUTTERFLIES

walk with us in
evening light like children
who trust we know the way
and pause to explore
a twig
then dash to reunite till
a waving bough draws them off
to play.
Small and gold they pose on daisies.
Breaking up
their bloom they rise. Two touch
a third and fourth rush in to spiral..
Quickly chosen partners rest assured.
Folded on the road
they grant
a little space.

We turn
our shadows free from sun leap
fifteen feet ahead to nudge
just one.
In panic they all rise and flee

DESCENT

We do not sing as once we did
in solemn geometry
our purpled lilacs now glow white
against the sodden sky
and you in chilled wet stocking feet
descend by body weight
the roughened hill
to feel
the flourish of orchard petals
soon to expand
and solidify.

HAYSTACK

These hills all lay asleep. A snow
cover drawn from fence through field. I wait,
the darkened lambs below.
October clipped, time and weather create
their coats of wool-stained umber.
Black ears and legs in count locate
individuals in shifting number
pressed to the mushroomed bale of hay.
Dampness and wear have eroded the amber
harvest sheep focus on each day.
Its deepening carpet and shelter soft, as
breath melts icy bite away
detaching sheep for winter's dramas
as final twigs of forage pass.